Contents

Our smelly world

Smell is one of the five senses. Our senses tell us things about the world around us.

Our five senses are hearing, sight, smell, taste and touch.

We use our sense of smell when we cook food.

OUR FIVE SENSES

Smell

Sally Morgan

Explore the world with **Popcorn** - your complete first non-fiction library.

Look out for more titles in the **Popcorn** range. All books have the same format of simple text and awesome images. Text is carefully matched to the pictures to help readers to identify and understand key vocabulary.
www.waylandbooks.co.uk/popcorn

First published in 2013 by Wayland
Copyright © Wayland 2013

Wayland
Hachette Children's Books
338 Euston Road
London NW1 3BH

Wayland Australia
Level 17/207 Kent Street
Sydney NSW 2000

Editor: Nicola Edwards
Designer: Robert Walster
Picture researcher: Shelley Noronha
Series consultant: Kate Ruttle
Design concept: Paul Cherrill

British Library Cataloguing in Publication Data
Morgan, Sally
  Smell. - (Popcorn. Five senses)
  1. Smell - Juvenile literature
I. Title
612.8'6
ISBN: 978 0 7502 7859 1

10 9 8 7 6 5 4 3 2 1

Printed and bound in China

Wayland is a division of Hachette Children's Books, an Hachette UK Company
www.hachette.co.uk

Photographs:
Cover, 4 Blend Images/ImagePick; title page, 5 Tina Lorien/istock; 2, 12 © Sean Justice/Corbis; 6 Ecoscene/Chinch Gryniewicz; 7 © Birgid Allig/zefa/Corbis; 8 © Adrian Muttitt/Alamy; 9 © Creasource/Corbis; Shutterstock/ZQFotography; 11 Vasko Miokovic/istock; 12 © Sean Justice/Corbis; 13 Ryan McVay/Getty; 14 Code Red, George Hall/Getty; 15 Ecoscene/Robert Pickett; 16 Ecoscene/Bruan Cushing; 17 Ecoscene/ Robert Pickett; 18 Ecoscene/Satyendra Tiwari; 19 David Tipling/naturepl.com; 20 © Anna Clopet/Corbis; 21 Billy Hustace/Getty; 22 Martyn f. Chillmaid; 23l Christian Weibell/istock; 23r Roman Pavlyuk/istock

Some things, such as clean clothes and scented flowers, have a pleasant smell. Other things, such as rotting food and rubbish on the street, smell horrible.

Some flowers give off a strong scent.

Noses

Noses vary in shape. There are long noses, short noses, wide noses and turned up noses! What shape is your nose?

How would you describe the shape of these noses?

6

You have a nose with two openings called nostrils. You smell by breathing in through your nostrils. Stand outside and sniff the air. What can you smell?

Words you can use to describe smells include: clean, fresh, musty, sharp, sweet, sour.

Imagine you are sniffing these towels. What might they smell like?

How do we smell?

Smells travel through the air to your nose. The smells tickle special detectors inside your nose. These send messages to your brain so that you can identify the smell.

We feel hungry when we smell food being cooked.

Perfume has a pleasant smell. When we spray perfume, tiny droplets of it float around in the air. The droplets travel through the air into the nose.

Food and smell

Smell helps us to decide if food is good to eat. A lovely smell makes us want to eat something.

We can use our sense of smell to check if a pineapple is ripe.

A bad smell stops us from eating some foods. It is a warning that they will taste horrible and might make us ill.

Fresh bread smells sweet but bread that smells sour and mouldy is not safe to eat.

Milk that has gone off smells bad.

Smell and taste

Your senses of smell and taste work together. You sniff food before you put it in your mouth. As you chew your food, smells travel upwards into the back of your nose.

These cakes smell good enough to eat!

When you have a cold, your nose gets blocked. You cannot breathe through your nose, so you cannot taste your food.

Can you taste food when you hold your nose?

Warning smells

Some smells are warnings. The gas that we use for heating and cooking has a smell added to it. This means we can smell the gas if it escapes.

We smell smoke and flames before we see them.

Some animals release strong smells. Often this is a warning to other animals to stay away.

If people or other animals come too close to a skunk, it sprays them with a revolting smelly liquid.

Some animals release smells to attract other animals.

Animal noses

Animals have a sense of smell, too. Many, such as horses, dogs and cats, use their noses for smelling.

The proboscis monkey has a very long nose.

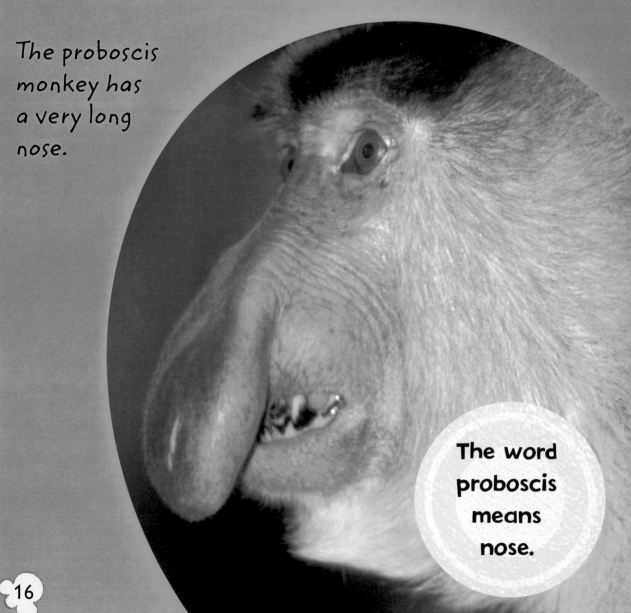

The word proboscis means nose.

Some animals smell with other parts of their bodies. Snakes have nostrils, but they smell with their tongue.

This snake flicks out its tongue to smell its surroundings.

Animals and smell

Animals use their noses to find food or to find their way home. Some animals hunt other animals by following their smell.

This tiger is smelling the tree trunk to pick up the scent of other animals.

Many animals know their young by their smell. Each animal's young has a smell that is different from all the other young animals.

Mother seals use smell to find their pups.

Expert sniffers

Some people have a really good sense of smell. They may be able to tell the difference between as many as 10,000 different smells.

Perfume makers need an excellent sense of smell.

Many animals have a better sense of smell than people. Dogs have large nostrils and many smell detectors in their nose.

A sniffer dog at work.

Sniffer dogs are trained to find explosives and drugs by their smell.

Make a smelly pizza!

Choose some smelly pizza toppings such as blue cheese, anchovies, olives, spicy sausage, smoked bacon and onion.

Now build your pizza. First spread the tomato paste over the base. Then add your toppings. Lastly grate some mozzarella cheese on top.

Now ask an adult to cook the pizza for you.

When the cooked pizza has cooled slightly, do a smell test. Do the cooked toppings smell different from before?

Finally do a taste test!

You will need:
- a ready-made pizza base
- tomato paste
- mozzarella cheese
- a selection of smelly toppings.

What's your favourite smell?

Often we link a smell with a memory. Have you ever visited a beach and smelled the sea? Perhaps you have visited a farm and remember the different animal smells.

Try to remember the smells of the different places you have visited. Can you describe the smells?

Glossary

brain the control centre of the body, found inside the head

detectors things that detect that something is there

expert knowing a lot about a subject, or having a special skill

nostrils openings in the nose

rotting decaying

scented having a smell

senses functions of the body through which we gather information about our surroundings

sniffer dogs dogs that are trained to find things such as drugs by their smell

Index